When I Wear Bob Kaufman's Eyes

by

Tom Murphy

When I Wear Bob Kaufman's Eyes
© Copyright 2022 by Thomas Michael Murphy

Gnashing Teeth Publishing
242 E Main St
Norman AR 71960

Cover Design and Artwork: Mot, and Marj Green

The cover font is Montserrat and Magenta Rose

The interior font is Garamond

Printed in the United States of America.

ISBN: 979-8-9854833-4-5

A Gnashing Teeth Publishing First Edition

GNASHING TEETH

PUBLISHING
words that get in your teeth

Praise for *When I Wear Bob Kaufman's Eyes*

When I Wear Bob Kaufman's Eyes is an intimate poetry of witness, a celebration of nature, language, and art. Lush yet economical, piercing, it explores breath and space, the verse is often projective. In a painful and playful study of experience, an elegiac reverie never forgetting a mission to testify what love and peace have met in conflict, in America, Tom Murphy is injured, angered, and still transcendent. He offers us a forgiving embrace of culture, a world in crisis. He introduces us to the characters that inform our everyday, a journal poet serving up a daily dreambook, never shying away from the nightmare, reminding us "our/brok en/ hi story, /mir rors/ u s." This is poetry of the 21st Century, we do not drown in aesthetics or appeasement. There is a strong personal voice that pummels through abstraction, seizes the unknowable and the unanswerable, through the magic of juxtaposition, and awakens and heals. In this book of poems there is a narrative that embraces truth, and beauty is there all along or arrives before we know it. This book is a life.

—Michael Rothenberg, co-founder of 100 Thousand Poets for Change. Author of *Wildflowers for The Bullies* and *In Memory of a Banyan Tree*. Rothenberg is the Florida State University Libraries Poet-in-Residence

Tom Murphy knew Bob Kaufman through his poetry, his story, and through mutual friends. He was so impressed by Kaufman's words that he used the following quote as an epigram for a chapbook:

> The poet shocks those
> around him. He speaks openly
> of what authority has deemed
> unspeakable. He becomes the
> enemy of authority. While the
> poet lives, authority
> dies. His poem is
> forever.

In *When I Wear Bob Kaufman's Eyes*, Tom does indeed view the world through Kaufman's eyes, and what he sees is self-interest, duplicity, bigotry, violence, and greed. Like Kaufman before him, Tom becomes the enemy of corrupt authority – exposing the bloated underbelly of society to the teeth and claws of poetic scrutiny. His words resonate with passionate and head-spinning honesty. He prods our awareness. He challenges our sensibilities. His images vibrate. His words fire our very nerve endings.

Ann Howells, author of *Painting the Pinwheel Sky* and *So Long As We Speak Their Names*

Between these covers you'll hear echoes of Yeats, Ginsberg, and of course Kaufman, woven together in a voice that is uniquely Tom Murphy. Whether he's taking you up a sagebrush plateau, to a winery in the French countryside or, musing on a most unconventional Ash Wednesday, Murphy's poetry exhibits the best of the Beat tradition, but moves well-beyond, displaying a mastery of sonics, an ability to gild the familiar image with unconventional profundity that is unparalleled. Part Cheshire Cat, part Caterpillar, Murphy is exhaustingly exhilarating; leaves you wanting to blaze up a post-coital smoke. Yes, we may be looking through Bob Kaufman's eyes, but the vision shared is Murphy's and Murphy's alone.

Paul Juhasz, author of *The Inner Life of Comics*

A book informed by San Francisco, Bob Kaufman, Black Mountain poetics, friendships, and important mentors and poet teachers. A wondrous homage unflinching, and memoiristic, *When I Wear Bob Kaufman's Eyes* is both romping and serious in its outlooks. Here the poems speak of love and survival scrutinizes white supremacy and state violence, and converses with the dead poetry, place, in an exploration of a life of the poetic imagination. A wondrous record of the times.

--Hoa Nguyen, author of *A Thousand Times You Lose Your Treasure*

Contents

Bomb   Kauf   Whirl

Cirrus Wisps Reel

Bob Kaufman

While reading *The Collected Poems of Bob Kaufman* in January of 2020, I recall Robert "Bob" Coleman-Senghor, my professor of Beat Literature at Sonoma State University in the mid 1990s, telling me about his encounters with Bob Kaufman in North Beach, San Francisco. Bob Coleman would offer to buy him food or coffee, but Bob Kaufman just wanted the money, although, both Bob's enjoyed talking with each other. They had more in common than their first names, both were African-Americans and both of them have played a pivotal part in my life. Sadly, both are deceased too young.

Although I never met him, I too had stories of Bob Kaufman. Mine began in the spring of 1986, when I was first starting at San Francisco State University working towards a Creative Writing degree, entering with my core curriculum completed at Foothill College in Los Altos Hills. I was twenty-three starting that January and I didn't know that Bob Kaufman had died on January 12, 1986. I was living with a Russian couple, Zoya and Lev, in Daly City. My first foray outside of the dwelling home in Barron Park. While failing all my classes that semester I learned an incredible amount of information through those classes and experiences. I learned of the Avant Gard through the Expatriate Writers of the 1920s in Paris that included all the arts taught by Robin Gajdusek. An incredible teacher that I later took his Hemingway course as well. But at the same time, I was still taking creative writing from Floyd Salas at Foothill College, in which Floyd and Claire Ortalda would drive Claire's small truck from Berkeley across the Bay Bridge and take I-380 to the I-280 interchange in Daly City and I would be waiting on the freeway bridge of the interchange and hop into the back of their truck for the ride to class. They thought I was a bit crazy to be on the intersection onramp like that, but it worked and it was very fast to get going quickly south the thirty-five miles.

Floyd's class saved me in so many ways. It was in his class that I found my writing voice. And in the spring of 1986, we were hard at work on putting out the Bay Area anthology, *Stories and Poems from Close to Home*. A massive 509-page tome that featured Czeslaw Milosz, Carolyn Kizer, Jack Micheline, Bob Kaufman, Robert Haas, Ismael Reed, Herbert Gold, Gerald Rosen, Gerald Haslam, Jonah Raskin, David Meltzer, Josephine Miles, Stan Rice, Eugene Ruggles, Thomas Sanchez, Nanos Valaoritis, Al Young, Julia Vinograd, Jerry Kamstra, Gary Soto, Leonard Gardner, and poets from San Quentin Federal Prison like Elmo Chapman, Coties Perry and Robert Day. I had three poems and a piece of prose in the anthology and was mentioned in the introduction as well. Rosen and Raskin ended up on my Master's Thesis committee at Sonoma State University.

It was on April 18th, a day after my twenty-fourth birthday, that I took BART from Daly City to the North Berkeley station and walked to Floyd's place. In Claire's front apartment, a little party took place with Floyd, Claire, Jack Micheline and his platinum blond girl friend, plus Lynne Wildey and myself to celebrate the release of *Close to Home*. Lynne told me that it was Bob Kaufman's birthday and he was in the book and had just died in January. She had been Bob's longtime lover. That moment was important to me. Bob's birthday and mine are a day apart and we were published together. My eyes were wide open during these times, making new connections and new ideas were bouncing around in my brain. It was in Floyd's Spring quarter class that started in late March of 1986 where I met my future wife, Susan Wolff. Married six years later and to the present we are together. Through the many readings to promote *Close to Home*, I met many brilliant writers including Lawrence Ferlinghetti at the City Lights reading, when Floyd gave a copy of the anthology to Lawrence that is now housed in the Ferlinghetti collection University of California's Bancroft Library. After the soiree in Claire's apartment, Jack Micheline and his girlfriend drove me to Café Babar in San Francisco's Mission District. That began a new introduction to open mic meeting other poets and reading there at Babar.

I read Bob Kaufman's poem "The Trip, Dharma Trip, Sangha Trip." I later bought *The Ancient Rain*, and *Solitudes Crowded with Loneliness*. I learned of Bob Kaufman's vow of silence from the assassination of John Fitzgerald Kennedy through the Vietnam Paris Peace Accord in 1973, in which he ended it by reading "All Those Ships That Never Sailed." What I did not know was that Bob Kaufman broke his vow of silence at the Palo Alto Art Center, where Susan and I were married in 1992. That information came from the fantastic *Collected Poems of Bob Kaufman*. Bob and I were published together again in *Beatitude: Golden Anniversary 1959-2009*. I had sent to Latif Harris, one of the editors, a four-page poem and somehow it got mixed up and he liked the first page and published that. I remembered buying *Beatitude: Silver Anniversary* and coveting that volume, other poets such as Curt Kline, who I had seen read at SOMA before, were in it as well. When I heard the call for poems for the *Golden Anniversary* edition, I sent in my poem. It was later on, even after the *Beatitude* anthology that I was able to buy *Golden Sardine* online. I've dipped in Kaufman's work over the years, but taught the three poems from *The Beat Reader*, especially his poem "On." In 2015, I used the following passage from Bob Kaufman's poem "The Poet" as an epigram for my chapbook *Horizon Horizon*:

THE POET SHOCKS THOSE
AROUND HIM. HE SPEAKS OPENLY
OF WHAT AUTHORITY HAS DEEMED
UNSPEAKABLE, HE BECOMES THE
ENEMY OF AUTHORITY. WHILE THE
POET LIVES, AUTHORITY
DIES. HIS POEM IS
FOREVER.

The Collected Poems of Bob Kaufman showcase an original voice, the pains of being an African-American and Jewish descent from his world-wide view from his travels as a Merchant Marine to his street scene living where he would rather have a room to stay than any books given him. Lynne Wildey told me that they were lovers and she was his woman when Bob Kaufman died. Then I learned in 1989 of Eileen Kaufman, Bob's wife. I met Jack Hershman at a party and picked up *Would You Wear My Eyes? A Tribute to Bob Kaufman* that is a beautiful and loving book. In that text, I saw Lynne and Bob and I saw Bob and Eileen and their son Parker. However, my favorite image was Ed Buryn's of Bob Kaufman leaping from a dumpster. Bob Kaufman, the black Rimbaud, lives through the pages of *The Collected Poems of Bob Kaufman*, his poem is forever.

Post Script: All but four poems in this collection were written between January 2020 and April 2022. Although, I did little to edit the original essay I penned, it amazes me how the essay and the poems seem interwoven, though that was done subconsciously. TM 7.10.22

In Memoriam
Floyd Salas (1931-2021)
Writer, Artist, Boxer, Teacher
A better mentor I could not have had

Bomb   Kauf   Whirl

Sagebrush Plateau

sagebrush plateau — a belt snaps on you
vortical swirl whirl tornado
rip chew chomp spew   sandy loam
                    red dirt
                    wood anything
arc path tattoo signature glyph on wold
howl moan trackless freight train anywhere
bite collect throw up turnabout toss out
swirl vortical whirl tornado
slap punch pulverize puncture pierce
                    what stands
                    what runs
                    what breathes
                    what caught
glyph arc signature tattoo path
shred shear shave shamble roustabout
lash pelt stomp ricochet smack
whirl swirl vortical tornado
embedded imprinted inlayed ingrained
sagebrush plateau   in your fears
                    in your mind
                    in your blood
                    in your bones

The Great American Windmill Bob Kaufman Destroyed

Not Wilhelmina's, south past the brewhaus   armless giant
wordhoard hacked away   splinter by splinter
Rimbaud stigmata pierced   eyes
stoned, giant's maimed roar   the surf
forever bellows—Tokáy bottle   hurl—
shatters silence to spew   All Those Ships
like wino in cell   3

Bob Kaufman would sleep   on broken slats
windmill arms, so   Jack Micheline
would bark at Cafe Babar   he said,
he was resting in the   giant's arms
that he slayed   snug as a
thug in a flood.   In Harold Norse's
cab backseat, Bob   died holding
a cross   voodoo menorah.

Three Staves

If I was ta'wil willing to please you
how much pleasure am I willing to give?

Time is everything.
How much am I willing to spend?

Even these words and lines are expenditures.
So, take them, claim them, as if I gave you gold.

But they will slide through your fingers,
poison your blood, slip away quicksilver.

Now alone in the dark waiting,
praying, for the brightening of stars.

Coffins have no windows through dirt.
Ashes float away, I'm alone in the ink.

Tuning

Listen to the color spectrum
unleash waves and particles
aural broad swaths
cantilever bombardment
stucco the museum mind;
just shuffle along, tuning.

Burnt Orange in C Minor
Seurat triplets Eb Ab and Bb
A fanfare breathing vermilion
into the Overture quartet
Clifford Still whole notes sustaining G
through Bb — Flaxen, Corn, Medallion
Bumblebee, Mustard, Tuscan Sun.
Cacophony of color
trills of Franz Kline
black clouds and lighting strikes
mellows to Barnett Newman's Stations
white   —   Jay DeFeo's tactile rose.
John Cage's 4:33—played a
plethora fan in the key of orange:
Sunrise, Candle Light, Orangutan, Melon,
Pumpkin, Papaya, Goldfish, Creamsicle,
Monarch, Ginger, Apricot, Salamander,
Basketball, Starfish, Tangerine, Mac and Cheese.

        Pin drops.

An aqua timber speaks,
"Color of the world,
this is Rothko Radio."

Through

Through time bond speed and propellent bounding through

On and on storefronts flashing through nothingness onward

Light came into being through kinetic cloud lightning

Electrical current fiberoptic whirls to ground electricity

Wire time together through networks of wirelessness

Synapses popping tandem synchronously snapping

Mindful thought spirals daily through series mindlessly

Memory stored deep databanks grey matter carries memories

Through days through nights hour by hour until through

Planes

planes
      d
        i
           v
             e
                      daily

in   the   s pace s

        over
            head

they are not
            my pro tec tors
they are not
            my friends

they are proof
            of money
they are proof
            of power
they are proof
            of con trol

they
      d
        i
           v
             e

to   keep me
   in   l
                    i
               n
                        e

Corpus Christi

Booze laden, you flock mask-less to your plastic strewn fecal tides
awaiting the resurrection or erection while crucifying your land corpse.

Your klieg lit benzine seepage flaring stacks of refinery desolation row
spread like COVID-19 around the bay to wink a multitude of Barad-dûr.

Steel pipe plants shed black dust transforming Portland into Pompeii.
        Your crop
lands — flood plains, now saturated DDT and Roundup converted
        track-housing.

Your fifty-year-old bridge you demand unworkable, indeed, for bigger cache-
        bound
zebra mussel tankers cannot reach your oily pipeline wells. Port Commission
        hires

proven contractor disaster, Floridian foot-bridge collapse-kills six. Idea
        blooms
like your illiteracy and teen pregnancy rates, a floating fuel dock at bay's
        mouth.

We guarantee no spillages—clean as a whistle! Cancerous, you watch
        loggerheads
and green turtles' bobbing empty shells that guide ships though oleaginous
        surf.

The latest Commission brainstorm—desalination. Desal plant on Harbor
        Island.
A maximum of ninety-seven million gallons of wastewater a day—only a
        trifle.

The aquifer mixed with Eagle Ford Shale fracking chemicals—nearly Death
        Valley,
but you, Corpus Christi—handout millions of gallons of water with cash
        bonuses

and tax exemptions to any willing multinational corporation to ransack and
pollute these once fertile lands. Your pocket payoffs for war machine
        military

madness and their toxic dumps, erecting statues, planes, and cemetery pit-
        plots
along with your proposed ginormous cross on I 37 where you will white-
        robe nail

as much of the land along with your AR15-style accumulated Blacks and
        Mexicans
to those grotesque beams that greet the future in a channel reek of infested
        sludge.

Sun Ra's racy dance

echo tide reverberating dawn sky

triskelion lion picks her teeth, eyeballing

next catch in coastal fog, trees, cypress,

redwood, mesquite, bent backwards, like

gimp at Barcelona's cathedral's unshaven legs.

Oh mama, frogs holding tacos in the air, why

do their medals hang sideways and swirl like

pasties in a hothouse bar? Sunlight dances over

hands unfit to shovel graves, but blisters pop

and burn. Did you see the coming garbage trucks?

How do you put your pants on when you're still

fetal bed dreaming viscous scenes of death?

I don't know

I don't know
        how far out
                is out there
don't know   don't know

tongue and groove
        tool and die
                John and Merce

far out   not out there   no look leapt

they're out,
        far out,
            past the Be-In

leapt in the 40s dropped in their 20s

musical patterns
        riffs, triplets
              double trio

dissonance
        improvisational
            siren wail
                tinkling glass

gurgling toilet
        water & pipes
                bubbling bong
rustling
     rustling cows
       rustling paper
           paper cut,
              cut out the

Mercy float of Candlemas fair.
        Leapt.
           Float out

       got off

          on / off

             the bus

                 high water mark

moment too far out

       out for a while

             not out of it

                 not

recover undercover lover

       out beyond there

             tool and

                 groove

tongue and die

       pimp and John

             Ho Ho

                 Ho

out of bounds

       out of relief

             out of time

               out of

                 habit

she drew the blinds

       out of light

             out of energy

               out of

                 night

out beyond dawn

       out beyond stick figures

               placing

                 pennies

on their eyes,

       on the piano strings

               bolt cutters

tuning interdimensional

       yoke and yak

             out

               out there

leapt and leapt

       leaping still

             jar to jar,

               falling

                                                still
one hand trap
            ripe ripped
                    offed offer
                        out
                                outed
they're there
            their out—there
                        unaware
                            of wavelength
                                    oscillation
pounding
            Fenollosaing
                    wave breakers
                            out there
wavelength
            breakers flipped
                        flugelhorn long
                                not
                                        e
flat far away,
            cresting crust out
                        their
                            Happening
                                            Ted
and Tom
            Hap
                    pen
                        ing   don't know
                                        how
out there
            they're
                    their
                        has become
keep on leaping
            keep on leaping
                        don't know tool &
                                        die
keep on keeping on
            far out
                    far out
                        don't know

tongue a

groove,

   Basa Nova,

    Samba,

     Fado,

      pinched strings

       John

        Cage

have mercy

  Merce Cunningham

    know how far out

      is out there

       pennywise

pennywhistle

   penny-farthing

     cycling

      Penny darling

marble corner

   cold as Olson's

     prose and

      pose topless

       great father

out there

   all-night obscura

     leapt Kerouac

leapt

   Colin Kaepernick —

     onto the playing field

  oddly uneven

    sphere of influence

 subjugation

    domination and

      discipline

  knelt at strains

    oh, can you

      feel the

       pain

Going to go to the mall

Pick up some pheno   barbital (sustain)

Check out the geeky girls' sustainability
Fast food choices—we've got antigay hillbillies

All I wanted was a Pepsi at the mall
For a good pick up, pheno   barbital (sustain)

Hundred dollar shoes and forever twenty-one skanks
Rather watch a run on the money that crashes banks

The internet is a tracking devise disguised as a mall
Gonna dive into the dark web for some pheno   barbital (sustain)

Out of the bars and into the streets, you cyberettes
They'll kick in your door for your stash in tin Clorets

Offer them a drink, when they toss your sprawl
Then take all your pheno   barbital (sustain)

Cubed Letters

Q is for queen
Queer
out spoken
silence equals death
P is for park
car park steam glass
Curious George Michael
toe tapping
en parcaque baño
X is for what he wanted
what we all wanted
sex
xo xo xo xo
kisses hugs
xx bang bang
T is for triangle
worn badge
Weimar Republic
goose step kicks
starving camps
showers of millions
burn to erase
the graphemes
from the pages of history
palimpsest
never completely gone
Blake's bones plowed under
Bucky Fuller adds a segment
tetrahedron strength

We Fight to Win

We work with fingers in the earth for mind breathes.
We work online prompts and vespetro meetings.
Dogs and cats our vesper through COVID-19 nights.
We are fighting for our lives —

Subtle loneliness creeps in — like a sweetly perfumed
beast laden with a blood-stained club fresh off the tanning bed
thumping our senses before pummeling our bodies
        — but we fight, we fight to win.

All our bad days, our catastrophes, our Black Sundays,
our days of infamy, our assassinations, our dropped towers,
our overrun sacred lands, our dragged into the streets
dead — leave us utterly forlorn.

But — this 'good earth' still rotates
        — spinning through space around a star.
We'll get off the floor, the couch and out into
that bright light to raise our voices to fight on.

For whom we fight? For the economy? *NO!* What is money
but a means of corrupt power. For the kids and grandkids.
The elderly who've been told to sacrifice their lives.
We fight for love and dignity; we will win.

Bomb Kauf Whirl

Plutarchian   Angels

                  whisper

on the sky bridge

                  overlooking

vast array of dumpsters

                  leapt from

Bob Kaufman crowded

                  in solitude

tears of cash corners

                  blinding light

Andy Warhol Race Riot (1964)

Four panel girdle man style
white wig with news print image

one black and white
                another blue
                            two red.

Black women and men
            lined up behind
            central image focus
            in front of trees
            staring
                    else where

What was missed here?
            Maybe they look
            to the future.

Maybe their vision
            sees
            Treyvon Martin
                        and
                            George Floyd
            screaming for life
                        before
                                silenced.

Maybe they see
            Barack Obama
                        as president.

Or Nixon declaring
                        war on drugs
            that makes it
            easier to haul them
                        away.

Maybe they see . . .

But their vision opaque by

the anger in the first cop's face
      as he let his dog
           rip through
                  trousers
                  flesh
      of a man

who is civil

who is tired
      tired of giving in

who drinks water
      while waiting in line to vote

who wants
      to run away

from the snapping
           jaws

of German shepherds
      but refuses and stands.

Warhol's newspaper images
      captures whitey's sickness

that pervades America—
      its whole life—still.

4'33" Revisited

metal magnetism   pure chance

                                                            luck

random acts that may have been, might have

                                                            been

annotated by fellows, gal like gallic tides

                                                            weave

spiraling downward, symmetrical gauging inward

                                                            here

there and every time change, Tao thinking

                                                            who

placed the chairs? Ionesco wasn't there. Cut-up

                                                            Yoko

couldn't make it but she sent airmail email

                                                            love

mail to John. Who placed the chairs? Hall

                                                            chairs

lined up for the exhibition, BMC. Bowel

                                                            movement

collective must of been a joke, shepherds,

                                                            tongue

and groovers, mercurial churchicals,

                                                            provo-

cateurs, riches to rags. Black Mountain

                                                            College

shoveling dirt, democratize. Hung sweat

                                                            Asawa

weaving with wire, with MC, with Hazel

                                                            Larson

wheeling crutches, I-Ching John to Tite

                                                            leap

then look, take the chance. Yoko sends love to

                                                            John

Cage. Seat, told while we sat, in BMC

                                                            Museum

Broadway stilted sculpture outside, how

                                                            random

the chairs were set. "Pack 'em in," our

                                                            cage

around inside out artifacts. Oh don't mind,

never

think, let it happen, be in, happening.

Asawa

hangs, woven, hang-about Blake Arkansas

light

dimmed for internment barbed wire, mushroom

pickers

before face masks, death masks, masquerades

faux

ever the moment to be in. There the chairs

set,

he sat, he leaned, he leapt, Asawa leaned

in

cageing him, the imbecilic mook chairback

muck

Hazel's boot across the veil, magnetism

negat-

-ive shot across Eden, light just so's leap

hung

airborne, through the print missing limbs

weft

thin air, dancing on the potter's wheel,

lowing

cows on the breeze, on the floor, crimping

deft

hands pull gauge of gage in study building,

Cage

at dinning hall piano, pennies on the

carbon

steel strings, mercifully dancing across the

keys

from the bench, a chair, set for performance

BMC

M+AC, Broadway stilted space, Highland

brews

iced given away, Asawa strung hung gauge

steel

weave, chairs too close, Asawa leaned in,

ignorant

chair dweller leaned back, Cage lecture

2011

night, bouncing off Asawa warp and woof

                                    Toluca

Native learned, steel to hair, chair to strands,

                                    rattle

a note came to be so random, clear tone rang

                                    free

On the Death of Lawrence Ferlinghetti at 101

Blindsided
straight to *Americus* Book I
bandy-legged and gender-blended
then the Krishna gave me three books
thinking I was enlightened.
"Where did you hear about us?"
A million thoughts raced
into airports.
"We cannot wear our robes here."
Vishnu and Homer
the dog
taking on the cops
micturated on
one at a time.

Whirlwind day
Covid days we're living in.
Breath release
hoping another comes.
Will the Krishna
whom gave away books
still find their passion
unskewed after reading
A Coney Island of the Mind?

When I Wear Bob Kaufman's Eyes

pillows become marbleized pillars
        of tiger's teeth.

When I wear Bob Kaufman's eyes
polar bears drown in tar, singing
raga dirges until noxious fumes
stream green from their pointy ears.

When I wear Bob Kaufman's eyes
homeless shelter bunks swallow lonely
children, by morning only their skeletons
are left chattering.

When I wear Bob Kaufman's eyes
Hiroshima light bulbs pop around the
globe in cut time to signal SOS.

Again

(sotto voce)

No matter the car, plush or beat, scared to death to drive that road of life
going below the speed limit. As you pass them by, you notice the driver is
a person of color going the maximum of the law, not because they believe
    it's
their citizen duty to obey the law; they are scared to death of the cops, again.

Klan cops, QAnon cops, proud boy cops, vigilante cops, peckerwood cops,
    rent-a-pigs.
They're not pseudo empathetic actors in TV shows or in flicks trying to
    convince you
what holy sanctified goody good law-abiding people they are that you should
    trust—
they're the pigs who put up signs to be out of town by sunset, again. The
    cops that cuff you

for nothing, again. The cops that plant drugs in people's pockets, in car's
    gloveboxes,
in home air ducts or under the couch cushions. The cops that take your coke
    then whip
out a mirror from their uniform breast pocket in the squad car as if they
    always carry
a mirror, again. Those pigs that arrest wheelchair bound people, ripping apart
    their chair,

bashing-beating those who try to help the invalid with chair parts, again. The
    pigs that
beat you senseless, again. Beaten in squad rooms like Jonah Raskin, again.
    The pigs
that leave you bleeding to death on the streets to die, again. Those pigs that
    pull you
over for too loud music in stop and go traffic in Los Gatos, when you jump
    out

to take their picture, they threaten to beat you at the station house; or the
    FBI tailing
you, to corner you at home for your epistolary articulated opinions; or when
    the pigs go
running through your gated yard, yelling they're on the chase and they as pigs
    have rights

to invade your privacy. So, lock your gates and your doors to keep the
motherfucking

pigs out of your house, again. Speed too fast, pulled over by the cops, asking
idiocy
with disdain wrath, packed with pepper spray, baton, stun-gun, extra
magazines with
pistol, wanting direction: "Where'd you come from? Where are you headed?
Did you know
you were going too fast? Do you have insurance? Do you have a license? Do
you want me

to take you downtown?" again. Pigs pulled over a brown or black driver,
giving them the
once over with siren flashing lights, hand on gun, dragging them out of the
car, bent over
the hood and cuffed, again. Passing by the wallowing pig who bellows his
baton shit, I yell,
"Racist citation!" again. The ghost of Gil Scott-Heron rises and says, "They
want to send whitey

to the moon," again. Whereas pigs' knees on necks killing in the name of
their trumped-up
fake warrants no knock break in with shotgun shooting unarmed sleeping
women in bed,
again. Louisville's gas-masked horseback police in 2004, San Francisco's
1984 Democratic
Convention Civic Center protest, swinging down their skull-cracking
truncheons, again.

Swinging batons at anyone in their way, beating anyone down on the ground
to a bloody
pulp as if they have the right to kill those non-threatening people, again.
Marching in full
riot gear, down Berkeley's University Avenue, during the Battle of Seattle,
through Joplin,
through Minneapolis, through Kenosha, through Sanford, through Ferguson
through

Portland, through Charlottesville, through Oakland, through Anaheim,
through Milwaukee

through St. Louis, through New York City, and down your street, Barron
    Avenue, through
your neighborhood, your burg, town, city metropolis, slam dance
    cosmopolis, again. Again.
Pigs killing, again. Again. Again. Pigs killing, again. Again. Again. Pigs killing,
    again. Again. Again.

H. Hattie (for Tom Clark)

Ruminate on Hanover Hattie, tunnel foreword —

Sky orange marmalade with Saint John akimbo

Swingline buzz the death of "I" across the circle

Estrella gaze fog breath after a June snow

Hottub Hattie slips over the boarder for a soak

Ferryman JP2's frog voice from esophageal cancer

Midstream announces that Tom Clark's onboard for the ride

Who when called upon stood to yell, "This isn't Berkeley!"

Hulu Hattie podcasts, "Charles & Ed want a word or two."

Ponder each grapheme, my good god that's a load of gravel

Oil rigs bleed the Permian with a chock hold frack

Breath mint Jo Jo over sows the cheeky support of bangtail

Gas-dip by psalms on Corpus Christi unqualified Cruz

Shrill flatness tarnished the House of Rock with Cubism (illegitimacy)

Reduction plasma extractor nightwear breechcloth

"Posterity," screamed old-line Cyclops midriff sallow six-pack

Pseudo Machiavellianism yellow shiftiness nausea puke

High-Hattiness swellhead braggadocios flaccidness

Hoity-toity criminal diabolic rash crave purple charge

Roebuck rackabones sucking up chokeberry soup rouge

Nonconduction frequency semidarkness patchwork dirge

Heavyhearted Hattie sourpuss laments Tom's specter

Swantner Park

Corpus wind bent palms as I cross Ocean
                                            [Drive.
Along the NW seawall he came from the carpark
weaving through vehicles in motion stationary. Heading SE.
He was an artist, T— V. I knew by sight though never
having any real conversation except pleasantries in mixed
company. Head switching over shoulder, as if something followed
him in the flecked cloud wind. Charging forward as I meander.

Blvd up hill to the left. Bay to the right. Whitecaps slapping the
seawall steps vigorously. At a moment, ten or so paces away,
I caught his eye and hold its glance and his head rises
                                           [skyward
Then eyes come down to me and takes leaping steps towards
                                           [mine
We stop. Simultaneously, nothing planned. Simpatico.
I notice the charcoal smudged smock and graphite in his right hand
                                           [clutched
tightly. He raises the right hand and twirls air circle
marks or chicken scratching that I cannot ascertain,
but they were continuous motions some more striking,
some softer in their motion
                                   then stops.
He turns abruptly. Storms off. Leaving the way he had
come. Nobody up by the Blvd. I look back to the blue
water and the sea steps, not even gulls.

I follow him, hitting Ocean and turn
                                         [home.

Man

I saw a man's bone
saw it sticking out his leg, man

I saw a bone, man
I saw a bone, man

      bone s aw man
every prince needs one, man

I saw my bone, man
I saw my bone, man

      bon soir, man
      bone saw, man

ochre-red lead-white blood calcite echoing s
                             cream, man
nevermind quadrophenia tonight's the night r
                     aw power, man

I saw a bone, man, on TV, man
slo-mo five six seventeen youtube times, man

ankle dislocation tibia fibula lacerated skin, man
May Be Sure, MBS no longer sooner needs, man

      bone saw man
Hagia Sophia Cisterna Basilica Dardanelles spicy market

Khashoggi-man scattered wind Aeolus blown
white vans around — I saw a bone, man

I saw a bone, man, I saw a bone, man
I saw a bone, I saw a bone, I saw

bonesawman

Ash   Wednesday

Five of us were on BART
under the San Francisco Bay
zipping along towards Oakland
holding a stainless-steel pole
when we dropped acid.

         Matt didn't couldn't wouldn't go
         to experience the Dead. I did and paid
         for a ticket and would take 18 MUNI
         from Westlake Daly City, where I lived
         with Russians, Zoya and Lev Rosenburg.

I talked about the writers and artists of Paris
twenties, their inventiveness of those expatriates.
Will called them, the Avant Garde, a new term
to my mind on Ash Wednesday, 1986. My senses
were so in tune with that bright light of his eyes.

         Matt introduced me to Shelley and
         Daniel, their apartment over looked
         Geary Street in the outer Richmond
         the weekend before the show
         Matt had the hots for Shelley—

         Microphone stand city at the back floor
         for anyone to record the night's offering from
         Bobby, Phil, Mickey, Brent and Jerry Garcia.
         In floor curves, couples danced fast; never saw
         bodies so in tune with each other's writhing grooves.

After the Neville Brothers jam, people
in the outer walkway, fifty or so Deadheads
sitting in circles passing joints shirtless,
tripping topless chillaxed ready for the band,
we three hit the packed bar for a quick drink.

         and Will came over later, nobody had
         really slept. Justine and Will drew
         painted through dusky dark early hours
         of the night until passing out. Paint
         caked hands grotesque like dried blood

Justine asked, if I was gay? Back in the seats between us,
Do I only like men? The gin and tonic a ton of bricks,
light tracers arc as Justine berated my sexuality brutally.
I looked at Will's questioning, he couldn't hear her.
Justine such a real bummer, but she wanted me.

Shaken, stirred, I floated downstairs and onto the floor. He
was tall even sitting and reached a joint backwards that I took
and toked, sat down, whipped out my clay pipe to share hash
with my new friend. The band began to tune on stage and we
stood for them to start. Ochre yellow floor, floodlight tracers.

Justine's first floor hazmat mold apartment
I hadn't seen it that evening, but spent spring
nights later rendering her animalist tones.
Parents older, richer, lived in Hillsborough
I never met them; she was too damn bossy.

The tall guy's pinball eyes stared at me
he emitted a sound like a plane's bombing raid
as "Hell in a bucket" kicked off, I started
peaking. Bobby Weirs' head began to burn
and his skull fully emerged from his skin.

Somehow the five of us made it back
to the outer Richmond where I tried to sleep
on the couch when I finally came down
by smoking ochre yellow hash. Daniel
brewed coffee while Shelley slept. Justine

We stumbled to a video rental store
picked up two flicks I'd never before seen
Eraserhead stomping on the falling worms
The Thing morphing alien into killer dogs
until blowing Antarctica station into oblivion

Bobby's fire red laser beam eyes saw my dad trying to choke me
to death, "At least I'll enjoy the ride." Hatchet in my hand I struck
dad, his yellow blood flowed, covering the floor "Ride. Ride."

I fully understand the existential moment
the lights and the swing, stoned
right then and there
"Shake it, Shake it, Sugaree."
the vision's meaning
free to be myself
driving from Ketcham across Idaho at 100 mph
"Fire on the Mountain" cranked up, drinking St.
Stan's Altbier snatched from the cooler,
passing
everybody on the way
to Craters of the Moon.

Ninety-Eight

Ninety-eight?
     What? Degrees?   That's good.
Brooks County—   Death Valley
     What?   La Migra
  Those piss ant motherfuckers
  slicing water bottles
     dashing food supplies!
¡Noventa y ocho!
     Demasiado
               pasaron
     No es suficiente
Demasiando muertos
Sangre en sus manos
     La Migra
Estados Unidos
Sangre en sus manos
Noventa y ocho
¡Déjalos estar en paz!
     Paz amigas y amigos
       Paz.

Patina Broken Obelisk

Patina
broken obelisk
not Barret Newman's.
Another, small in a glass case.
The patina, a greening of bronze,
induced rather than naturally aged
unlike the Statue of Liberty

s

he

ar

ed

top pinnacle angle
pentagram sides with a triple base
as if a model of time's fleetingness.
Some may say you are a male metaphor,
masculinity lopped in our day and age.
Though Avebury Henge's obelisk was ruled by women.

Stu
dent
of
art
What was your purpose, your intent?
Never completed form though form has always been
complete. A miniature pike unlike any other with five sides
like a cenotaph of war dead that could not hold a promise—
never sending out the youth into the too well-known slaughter.

De   form   ed
obe   lisk,
our
brok   en
hi story,
mir rors
u s.

Virago

Your clairaudience
hears baited breath
not pranayama.

Algid greeting
embranglement family
diurnal worry

non calescent
potential unwavers
luckless aleatoric

caliginous thought
sanguineous deracination
incalculable schismatic.

Wheatfields

> "Maybe I wanna see the wheatfields
> over Kiev and down to the sea." *The Call Up* by The Clash

Russia invaded Ukraine
wanting Zelensky's head.
Putin story trumped up.
Exodus into Poland, Romania, Bulgaria
far away out number Belarus and Russia.

Mr. Fuckface Putin,
I now address you,
put on your shirt
    and die.

Death follows you everywhere,
unlike snow, the sobs and wails
reverberate a cacophony of sorrow.
Slip Novichok into his vodka,
water or just give him an enema
with the nerve agent.
Youtube his foaming mouth
wide eyed whites.

What a sweet perfume;
      wheat waves.

Cirrus Wisps Reel

Dear Vaccine,

spread your juice into the world's veins
convince those that believe they're getting a computer chip
lodged into their brains from Bill Gates that it is still better
to be alive than dead and processor-less in these overwhelming times

Living, Teaching, Near the Water

Living, teaching, near the water
COVID-19 changed everything we know
Lectures on writing and slaughter

COVID cases front page blotter
Testing sites, obituary deaths grow
Masked up, quarantined near the water

Online PowerPoints, Harry Potter
Fear the card, Lightning Struck Tower hollo
Avada Kedavra slaughter

Twenty second handwash bother
Plexiglass hangs between computer row
Master says, "teach near the water"

Hate, riot guns, Black Lives Matter
Flatten the curve, Fakebook flambeau
President Trump's record slaughter

Patrick Dan, "Die for grand-daughter"
Refer container for body bags to stow
Gasping, dying, near the water
Corpus Christi led to slaughter

The Island of Jupiter

On the Bordeaux peninsula, we had stopped in Bordeaux properly, driven from San Sebastián, sitting outside of Saint Michel to figure our route on the newly acquired wine map, slowly driving north along the Garonne and decided to stop at Château Lynch-Bages. A fine Pauillac that we tasted in their stately château many different vintages of clarets. Leisurely, we meandered west to Benon and sought our night's stop. Le Bled campsite where old refrigerators were on their backside with doors removed for planter boxes; bean and tomato cages and lavender grew — cacti in toilets dot our garden now, was a bare-bones campsite, with a picnic table, a WC with shower, but no fire ring.

On our way to Pointe de Grave for the car ferry across Garonne to Royan and Chenonceau, we wanted to visit an artesian winery — a smaller château more local and less industrial. The map listed Château Laulan Ducos in the Medoc appellation, a little out of our direction. The owner, Francis Ducos, didn't speak English, although nice, alone, with no tasting room. Susan talked with the Vigneron in broken French and he was glad to share his laborious wines. We bought a bottle of each 1990 and 1991 vintages of his Insula Jovis — The Island of Jupiter. We hauled those bottles across Europe and home in the states and laid them down to age. That day with Mr. Ducos in his cluttered château as he worked hard to doll out his wares a sweet memory aroused with each cork popping, decanting and tasting years later.

Later, Château Laulan Ducos was purchased in 2011 by Richard Shen, the actor Shen Dongjun of the Chinese Jewelry chain store TESiRO, now called Leysen that has four hundred stores, where bottles of Insula Jovis will be sold, using the face of actress Zhang Ziyi of *The Wasted Times*.

> centuries old vines
> Medoc artesian claret
> honeymoon palate

Endurance

While watching the film *The Seagull*,
based upon Anton Chekhov's play
which I haven't read, my bad!

the word "endurance" clicked
my brain. In our time it will be
endurance that will get us through

the days and nights of self-isolation.
Shielded from the many voiced crowd.
The classes of students that diligently

search the texts for empathy
and ethics of care. The people
of Art Walk that drift around

K Space with a glass of wine in hand
to view the amazing art like Jimmy
Peña's 100 Portraits in a Year. Or

those who clink glasses after they pour a
favorite brew at the beer share. The gatherings
with friends at the Executive Surf Club,

Rebel Toad taproom, Scuttlebutts, The Post,
Tannins, BKK, and Snoopy's Pier. The Open
Mics at Del Mar College, Graffitis Downtown

The Exchange, and Bella la Brew. The casual
get together at Acapulco's on McArdle with El
Profesor or with colleagues at Driftwood Coffee or the

Tertulia with poets at Nick's home. The run-in
with friends unseen for ages at HEB or even
those you wish to avoid. The bustle on the

Island University, where greetings from students,
staff and faculty enliven an inner peace. Stopping
to talk to a former student, whose name slips

through the cracks like gold in *Paint Your Wagon*,
tells you they are graduating at the end of the term
in a field far from your own but their warmth

of heart so bright you wish them all the best
of luck and congratulations. Now, plans have
changed with endurance. Up before five for

toilet paper, garlic and the cat food case of
cans with pate with sauce and that treasure
that has been missing but shelved in the middle

of the night, because truckers still drive and
stockers still stock. Norman Mailer said
in the late 80s that when he was writing

his life was like a monk's, alone, solitary.
Of course, that was after his wild and crazy
party years where he was slipped the knife.

Our endurance must be acted as slow burning.
To endure the incessant waves of panic that
proceed waves of virus and waves of death.

Endurance, my friend, is your friend indeed.

Lights on the Billboard

Lights on the billboard went out
orange – purple clouds glowered dawn.
The sitting president is supine at Walter-Reed
infusion of designer drugs courses his veins.
Lincoln said, "Play Dixie, it's ours now."
Strike up a dirge and let that ragga drop
like a shelf of granite plunging down off Glacier Point,
bowling the forest down in a hundred-mile wind.

Democracy's death comes within a month from today.
His recovery, the Evangelical will declare a miracle.
"God has voted for us and we need not go to the polls.
Triumphant Trump should be president for life—
amend the constitution to make it so."
Here, sitting in a Waco hotel room with nowhere to go.

Lorca Vision

When I saw Lorca in a blinding light—
he smiled though the bullet holes bled
Flamenco guitar music slow duende dirge
      sing
ing, "Mi corazón se llena de agua"
"un solo pez en el agua" "y dos, y uno"
"Tenia la noche una hendidura" oozing
      snail
stepped, hands raised like Goya's "Third of May"
eyes closed as he Roma-swayed in place
he reached down and fingered the multitude,
      holes
in his torso when he begun Roma-stepping bare-
footed, feet balls side by side, heels hitting
turf, shaking his head, asking ¿Por que? ¿Por
      qué?
He was sucked back into the blackness of light
his hand extended towards me not as to reach
palm side up—as if el tranquilo barked, ¡Alto!

Market

Which market?
All American, Driftwood or Lucky's?
You broke your week streak
after berating the four of us
each day, even in the final moment
you in the driver's seat in full uniform
car running, heading to Twenty-Nine Palms,
I folding Sunday Chronicals on the front porch,
you lit me up with shaking rage.
Motoring off for a month after scoring
a few cartons, lighting the first one
the moment you passed that market door.

I'd bet on All American
since you drove by it to work
and closest. They didn't know you
none of the markets would recognize you.
It was folly to endure a week with
knowing you'd leave us for a month.
On return, happy as a clam, smoking—
                    all was forgiven.

Playing the Market

Bangtail over
place your wager
get your market share —
where will the military man
break his week long
cigarette fast?

All American Market — chalk to win
Lucky's Market — +300 money line
Driftwood Market — risk loving longshot
double zero — parlay all three Markets

Skill Prop bets —
1. Which market will be open on a Sunday morning
     at six am
2. Which direction would he access Bayshore Freeway
     a. Oregon Expressway
     b. San Antonio Road
3. Did he bring his week unused Zippo
     a. Or will he need matches
     b. Or use the car lighter
4. How many cigarettes smoked
     a. Before leaving market parking lot
     b. Before accessing Bayshore 101

Fun Prop bets —
1. Will there be an angry breakdown during transaction
     a. "Can't I get a goddamn smoke!"
2. Will he have to buy only packs instead of cartons
   Side bet —
     a. Quarters only in the machine –
          a. Will he drop one or more before getting first pack
          b. Before the second pack
          c. Before the third and fourth pack

There's money to be made!

Parlay — market, freeway access and cigarettes smoked
Accumulator actions before hitting the open road

dead dark thirty

In the Tenderloin
I got a London Fog coat.
He got a knife in his side.

I kept my job at the brewery
He lost it over a DUI;
but I talked too much on coke

threw me out of his and Billy's apartment
on Potrero Hill and I wandered
down to the Tenderloin.

Made friends with an old street man
                dead dark thirty.
He took me up to his sketchy hotel room.

He said he wasn't allowed guests.
"Quiet," he said, but the super knocked.
Up against the coats in Cracko's armoire.

"I told you to be quiet. You
like that coat? You look cold.
Take it man, but ya gotta leave."

Out the window down the fire escape
four floors and back onto the dark
Tenderloin skanky streets

nearing five and back to the brewery
for the early morning racking shift.
Drilling bung holes for Steam beer.

Healing

These hands are unfit to heal
What hands like these have wrought

In the mass shootings of Sutherland Springs
El Paso and Midland-Odessa

Burning hatred loaded guns
Blood in the pews   Blood in the aisles
Blood in the streets   Blood in our minds

Unlike Herostratus of Ephesus
Who burned the Temple of Artemis
Let us forget their names
Their weapons   Their angers
Let us celebrate the lives
                    Of their wrath

Let us remember Jordan Anchondo
               Who shielded her baby Paul
Let us remember
        The babies   The elderly
        The Mexicans   The children
        The lonely   The lovers
        The parents   The unborn
        Those that are gone
                           forever

Let us not forget that these murdered
        are us
Let us not forget to temper ourselves
        when life crumbles around our feet
Let us not forget to love
Let us not forget our hearts are stronger
        beating right now, to the rhythm of sorrow
        to the rhythm of joy
        to the rhythm of our joint presence
        to the rhythm of hope of a future

Our hearts and minds
Free of hands like these
Will help these hands become fit to heal

Pipestone

Pipestone soft stone
too many in Omaha are white
lots of Pride in Sioux Falls

non existences service at Motel 6
pool cover ripped with plants growing beneath
red nail polish like blood on the wall

no fridge or coffee maker
not even a cup or two
cigarette burns in duvet

no new towels for two days
the single garbage can overflow
pipestone burns for two poets

Janet

As you lay supine dying
from several immune diseases
will I make it to see you?
one last time

at Christmas, when our families gathered
in your Alameda homes or ours
in Barron Park, you and mom
would drink hot toddies.

Even before I can remember
you were present in my life
at a Murphy family reunion in Atherton
as a toddler – I jumped into a pool.

You thought I was all right
head and body bobbing along
but mouth and nose were under
you jumped in fully clothed to saved me.

We boys stayed a week years later
in Alameda where we went to the beach
multiple times, the only time I swam
the bay. My parents never reciprocated.

After dad died, you told me
you never liked him, bully of a man,
nasty and he never helped with his father
And he beat my mother with his killer fists.

We agreed on many levels.
I remember when he told your daughter,
my cousin, Joanna, that she had the
Murphy nose and she burst out crying.

Or when my dad refused to help cut up
his own father's meat at dinner in the
latter part of my schizophrenic grandfather's
life. Yes, dad did go with grandfather and his

half-brother Frank to San Francisco for
the 49ers-Philly game at Kezar; poor parking,
seagulls in the endzone puddles, but dad always
said they were no longer friends after grandfather

answered the door with a loaded 12 gauge
in dad's face, dragging dad indoors, barrels pressed
against his jaw. And dad remembered watching
his father shooting twenty clay skeets in a row.

No time for sudden movement — double barrel shot.
No, my grandfather and dad did not get along.
And you, Janet, his half sister-in-law
understood that my dad the colonel wasn't good.

As my brothers hide their shame
I speak out against bullies and abusers.

About the Mask

Only have one bought mask. The rest were given
and many home-made. Most of the given are too thin
as well as the bought, "You shall not pass!" Gandalf
mask with floating Covid-19 viruses battered back
by his staff on the Bridge of Khazad-Dûm.

Sarah, Gail and Janet hand sowed masks and gave
them away. The one that I use most come from Janet B.
Some rip my hair out, some burn the back of my ears.
Having to teach through them for classes face to face
while other students are synchronistical online —

fogging up glasses, feeling suffocated at times.
That one instant I appear without a mask, upon arrival
handed a paper medical turquoise one that hid my shame
from the tsk-tsk. For nine months so far with no end in sight.
I may not like wearing a mask, but I sure do love living.

Float in the Waves

Float in the waves of water
salted, speckled with plastic and tar
earthen humanized in its ruin.

Float in the waves of late afternoon
early October, water chill pushed by
Hurricane Delta to this shore.

Float in the waves as in utero
birth babies, like Britany's born Monday
live in embryonic fluid that seems close to water.

Float in the waves to relieve stress
take away these Covid-19 days, crazy Trump
and the year of 2020 before imploding.

Float in the waves looking skyward
pelicans in glide - search for fish to eat
cirrus wisps reel slowly free.

Float in the waves.
Float in water tonight.
Float away.

Pandemic Zoom

Pandemic Zoom —
we cower in our hovel
travel not out of Tejas
masked shopping in HEB
synchronous teaching veil.

Peel back
our shrouds, our
hearts into a wary
world of toads
in patio puddles.

Vaccination Insurrection.
Plans laid
flights arranged
rental truck,
hotels and car.

May, Palo Alto bountiful blooms
talked, listened, hugged.
Peninsula preserve hike — wild turkeys
strapping tape packed boxes
Napa Valley roam and sips.

Bed ridden Floyd Salas
poems read into ninety-year ears.
Chasborne helped, loading workbench
and chests, attaching truck tie downs.
Parched coastline lapping waves.

June, PW Covington — road trip
Burroughs' Lawrence Kansas home
Pride Parade in Sioux Falls
Pipestone quarry — soft stone spirit
the Falls, the reading, the stone, the pot.

July, Portugal plating on the periphery
Lisbon's narrow cobblestone street walk
Porto's rough river front almond tarts

Leiria's Jewish quarter meander
Atlantic beach friends and folly.

August, Malta's Valletta's grand harbor
ancient stone temples Ħaġar Qim and Ġgantija
bus and ferry ride to Gozo's shoreline
Victoria's majestic Citadel evenings
relaxing Black Cat Café cappuccinos.

Covid-19 killed four million and counting.
Time's wheels loosen isolation. Masks
and cleansed workspace still predicted.
I am no one who surveils the shadows
skulking survival mode — traveling.

Father

Albeit thin leather belt snapped
  hard on naked ass, the back-
handed face slaps, the punched
                    nose
wallops demoralized, Colonel's strong
  hands strangulated throat,
brown grey-flecked eyes burning
                    hate
  unnerved nearly passed out.
  Uncloaked Darth Vader, in a red
unraveled cable sweater, gray
                    slacks,
gold slippers, unshaven weekend
  anger for trifles, born (his word) pusillan-
mousiness tricksy from crushing
                    music
and hands, choking me with Victory
  at Sea on the box, the Black

Watch's Highland Pageantry on the
                    box,
Arthur Fielder's Motion Picture
  Classics on the box, the best
of Alfred Apaka on the box, mid
                  air
choking,
      gasping
          to

breathe.

Hard Travelin'

Earth has had some hard travelin' a late.
Tonga volcano eruption shock wave, interstellar
meteor slammed Papua New Guinea eight
years ago—Lord, how hard can relief be?

If this be livin', hard travelin'
is my life and times. Pluck me
a cord, Nathan or Woody, ride in
my car across this land to another

place where I can voice one more love
poem or truth exasperation. When it's
dark an' no light visible but stars—
hum a bar of Hard Travelin' Blues

before dawn melts my thoughts
with unbearable media-struck pain
around this earth comes to mind.
Bucha mass grave, women repeatedly raped

in old Ukraine. Deadly Afghan coal mines.
N train gassed and attempted gunned down lives.
Antarctic ice shelves collapsed, broke down into sea—
sustainability got harder travelin', Lord

for unionizing Starbucks and Amazon.
Quegqueg hard travelin' that Pequod
prow. Ahab called me Ismael, Lord
casket ocean bobbing, sunbaked, inside,

back skin bluer of my lover *George
Washington cannibalistically developed*, Lord
been havin' some hard travelin'—
vain is the insurrection over you.

Last Light Upstairs

Last light upstairs went out—
heart wrenching gait to the landing,
cold darkness, quietness beyond compare.
No bright wahoo, no sudden patter of feet,
squeal or laughter of youthful lives.

It comes parents, that loss, that
loneliness, that waver of wind that winds
our hair waiting for connection.
At times overwhelming,
at times too consuming,

at times all we lived for,
at times gave us comfort,
gave us meaning.
And like time, passes away with
the setting sun
        upstairs.

Education

Let us no longer build
but dismantle how they
                    l   earn,
throw away and discard pedagogy
you may have thought (wrongly)
                              wise
a good tool to use, that is no
longer important, then strip
                        piece
by piece apart, spread them out,
covering your desk, now dispel
                        each
component and let them drift
off your palette to slip into
                        gloom.

Sonnet 3 (for Susan)

I who meanders towards a final rest
Lilacs grow tendrils albeit not to bloom
Oljato pine's vanilla aroma
Sipapu whispers secret name on breeze
Happy Isles' cold babble sockless toe dip
Matadero's lush oak leaf duff crunch banks
Stand within the fin of Delicate Arch
Numerous paths I have yet to wander

Come hand in hand to view astonishment
A field of Indian blanket sways
Out double oven warmth comes sourdough
Our smart daughters, loving, and good people
Winter's cold brine rattles and razes roof
My chest your pillow as I hold you close

In Bone

The cold flames *en huesa*
Purple K retardant *vestido*
spots on the skin
veins popping through with map of
                                           blues
burning the body one byte at a moment
Baudelaire's "Carrion" splayed *polvo*
tireless worm the transformer

Pitfalls

Meander the pitfalls
   of our times
   masks on
   looking at friends
      wondering
         who have you
     been hanging out with?
     Do you talk to a buddy
     at HEB?
     Did you go to Lowes
     for roof caulking?
     Did you rub your eyes?
     Did you hug that friend
     getting a divorce
     like I did?

And the regrets
        mount like the corpses
        in the refrigerator containers
        will we see next year's dawns?
        staying home will only help.

Restless Man

A raised bed made with Elanor
three different soils mixed
basil, two types, oregano and
       a Roma tomato planted.

Clothes tumble in the drier drum
the cat whines for the tub water
pans clatter on stove coils with tapping
       of a wooden spoon.

If there is an act of sublime
it lies in the peace, tranquility
of the restless man who gets
       out of control.

Empty

Raked over the coals
sun dropped stone cold.

Day before yesterday's
tin can still empty

belly ache in a land of plenty.
Penned in for livin'

doing hard time, Lord —
my heart travelin' remote.

No control inside this porous
cyclone fence weary world.

Tales of love without
Kristeva, an open book of lies.

Ode to Joy less times starvin'
veggies and fruits rot on the vine.

Words are wonders when they make one smile
intonation can kill like a rattlesnake's bite.

Veins burnin' and heart's explodin'
more hard travelin' in a loveless zone.

America, get thee behind me —
gonna beg for a potato to eat tonight.

Memorial Day Weekend, 1990

Memorial Day Weekend, 1990
we re-met and crossed
the Santa Cruz Mountains
to stay in Half Moon Bay.

We laughed in the room
leaving nearly immediately
to pick up necessary
condoms to make the getaway.

We hadn't coupled in four
years and when we did
you wept after you came
then we spilled our hearts.

Marriage, children, being
a professor and growing
old together for the rest
of our communal lives.

The room was not enough
driving to Daly City cheap seats
to watch "Joe Versus the
Volcano." Crossing the Bay Bridge

to Oakland to hear Ismael
Reed read *Japanese by Spring*
from his own typed manuscript
near Jack London Square.

To hang out with Floyd
and Claire, to go back to
our room, miles away — you
listened to my cross-country trip.

Then we left together, though
you left town again, but
moved back in August to
travel across country too.

After you came back — our
Halloween dress up, you a
Cowgirl, me a Boy Scout
We moved in together in SF.

The Pipes

A sharp tongue big mouth asshole
have I been my whole life.

The near fights
        like the '81 Halloween costume party
        after she ripped my black hood off for the third time
        I slapped her beer cup from her hand
        dousing the dude she sat with who became enraged

        like the '88 New Year's Eve party in the Castro
        Leonard Gardner clasped my shirt front
        ready to punch but I mouthed off to a woman
        her man took over to grasp my shirt front

        talked my way out of being beaten to a pulp
        except the head smashed into a car window.

As a kid, Dad took us to see the Coldstream Guards
and the Black Watch at Oakland Coliseum twice
Dad bought a cantor and music book to learn to play
I said, I wanted to learn the pipes too—however his

cranking up bagpipe records after record full blast
during the weekend when he was miffed or drunk
came from his love of the pipes and having seen *Straw Dogs*
Peckinpah white noise ripping through neighborhood air.

A busker in San Francisco playing alto sax one eve
I tossed a twenty spot into his case and asked him
"Play Rachmaninov," laughed and walked away.
In Scotland, I always tossed five bob for women playing pipes.

In Inverness, I asked a male piper to play, "Cock
of the North," "I don't know that one."
"Play Scotland the Brave, laddie." Tossing twenty
pound note onto his black velvet on the concrete walk

from a story in *The General Danced at Dawn*
that my father relayed multiple times. "The Sergeant
Major said it was 'Cock of the North.' Everyone
knew if that Sergeant Major said so, it was true."

I like the pipes, I like the taste of scotch
I thought I had PTSD in Scotland when I heard
bagpipes playing, but the culprit was dear dead Dad.
My mouth got me in trouble, but I learned that sharp tongue

Nearly thirty years after his death, I am no
fighter and I keep my tongue on the page.

Sacredness of Life

Greed, money and guns.
They took what they could

        carry
bellies painfully empty already.
Some place had to be better.

        Estados
Unidos, el Norte, hermano y hermana.
What was another river to cross?

        Begging
all fourteen hundred miles
of walk. Chased by ICE. No

        money,
no food, no water. Ripped and
battered. Estados Unidos no

        bueno.
Hunkered under a mesquite tree, alone.
No God, no burning bush, no talking

        Snake.
Solo quiero una oportunidad.
Fathomless that in Estados

        Unidos
is greed

    money
guns

    and

        lies.

Seventeen

Crossing Huntington Lake
the Blue Bazoda's
wheel in hand
splish-splash wake
accompanies engine's roar

coming around Girl Scout Island

                     Eureka!

spotting the Jeffrey Pine
Oljato Pine
over seven hundred years old
sky deep as the blue water

such a young age
to shake loose
Plato's chains

Twilight of Stardust

left
sixty seasons
to farm
experts
      claim
our twilight
          stardust

crashing chaos
from here to
new maternity
       hello
echo —   good
           night
Irene — we have drowned

ourselves

choke
firelight air
red sun beat down

and *you* — want
to fund the pigs
follow hallow voices
         baby
shit's too real now
fan blades
in our face
      space
we need to find
to say adios
MF — melting away
        it's
twilight of
stardust
my friend
     breathe
from the O_2 tank
goggles on

swim thin light
                    soil
ready to give no more
nutrients depleted
hangman's gonna
                    swing
through death's door
those pearly gates false
human fatalities
                    Covid
disease — helps us
preserve all that we
stole — ready your
                    self
for the
underground

Peace

I want to make peace
      with the world,
but the world is not
      peaceable.

I spread my fingers
      in the sign of peace,
but the ripples are
      too short.

If we all do as
      Ringo Starr,
make the sign of peace
      together.

Maybe the ripples
      will create a wave.
Let us try
      together.

Everyone, make the peace
      symbol with your fingers.
Together.
      Repeat as I and Ringo say

Peace to the world.
Peace to the world.
      Peace.
      Peace out.

Acknowledgements

The author wishes to thank the following journals, magazines and anthologies for publishing the following poems:

Austin International Poetry Festival Digital: Living, Teaching, Near the Water
Boundless: The Great American Windmill Bob Kaufman Destroyed, Sacredness of Life, When I Wear Bob Kaufman's Eyes, We Fight to Win
Corpus Christi Writers: Endurance, Healing, Peace, Sun Ra's racy dance, twilight of stardust, Tuning
A Wreath of Golden Laurels: An Anthology of Poetry by 100 Poets Laureate: About the Mask
Good Cop/Bad Cop: An Anthology: Again (revised here)
Journal of Black Mountain College Studies: I don't know
Langdon Review of the Arts in Texas: Pandemic Zoom, Sagebrush Plateau, Three Staves, Through, Lorca Vision, Float in the Waves, Empty, dead dark thirty, Andy Warhol Race Riot, Sonnet 3, Father
Locust Review: Going to go to the mall, H. Hattie
MONO: Planes
Odes and Elegies: Eco-Poetry from the Texas Gulf Coast: Corpus Christi
Poetry is DEAD: An Inclusive Anthology of Deadhead Poetry: Ash Wednesday
Switchgrass Review: Janet
TX POETRY BALLOT: Lights on the Billboard
Voices de la Luna: Education
Wine: An Anthology: The Island of Jupiter (originally appeared as Tuesday Island)

This book could not have been generated without some rather important moments, books read, people and workshops.

The Great American Windmill Bob Kaufman Destroyed comes from reading Kaufman and living in San Francisco. The destroyed windmill in Golden Gate Park is the Murphy Windmill.
Three Staves owes credit to the Tarot Maximus workshop facilitated by Hoa Nguyen and Jeff Davis' presentation on Charles Olson and Ta'wil at 12 Re-Viewing BMC 2021 Conference in Asheville.
Sun Ra's racy dance came from the Duende Beat: Writing with Bob Kaufman workshop facilitated by Hoa Nguyen and Kristin Prevallet.
I don't know was influenced by Black Mountain College faculty and students, particularly John Cage and Merce Cunningham and the mantra

"Leap before you look." Ted Pope was also a major influence of this poem.

We Fight to Win, Hard Travelin', Empty are influenced by Woody Guthrie's music.

Andy Warhol Race Riot is an ekphrastic poem based upon Warhol's 1964 art piece.

4'33" Based upon John Cage's classic composition / theory. The event of the poem or "happening" took place at the 3rd Re-Viewing BMC Conference in 2011. Also, the poem mentions BMC alums Ruth Asawa, Hazel Larson and MC Richards, who I think were amazing artists.

On the Death of Lawrence Ferlinghetti at 101 italics a quote from *Americus Book I*, page 3.

Swantner Park again, from the Tarot Maximus workshop facilitated by Hoa Nguyen. The week before the workshop, I read the entire *Maximus Poems* by Charles Olson.

Man came from the Fred Wah's *Music at the Heart of Thinking* workshop facilitated by Hoa Nguyen. Plus, the horrific moments of the death of Jamal Khashoggi and Dak Prescott's extreme sports injury and the double compound fracture I experienced at fourteen.

Ash Wednesday influenced by the Grateful Dead and drugs.

Ninety-Eight the number of immigrants that died in the wilderness in south Texas in a month.

Living, Teaching, Near the Water, Education were both influenced from teaching at Texas A&M University-Corpus Christi during the Covid-19 pandemic.

Lorca Vision the italics are direct quotes of Federico García Lorca's poetry, but incoherently placed.

Father the poem's style and subject are heavily influenced by Nathaniel Mackey's *Double Trio* and *Breath and Precarity* which I read in 2021. *Double Trio* is also mentioned in *I don't know*.

Hard Travelin' italics from Herman Melville's *Moby Dick*.

Twilight of stardust contains lyrics from the song *Goodnight Irene*.

I would also like to thank Floyd Salas, Claire Ortalda, Hoa Nguyen, Michael Rothenberg, ire'ne lara silva, Carol Coffee Reposa, Gillian Conoley, Larry 'Buffalo' Thomas, Alan Berecka, Bill Mays, Robin Carstensen, Dylan Lopez, the PPF Committee, PW Covington, Edward Vidaurre, Nathan Brown, Ted Pope, Karen Cline-Tardiff, Stephen Wessells, Glenn Blalock, Pam Brouillard, David and Janet Blanke, Joe and Elisabeth Mermann-Jozwiak. I want to thank Paul Juhasz for not only writing a blurb, but for his exacting eyes and understanding when reading an earlier draft. I also want to thank Lori Atkins and the Bell Library Special Collections and Archives at Texas A&M University-Corpus Christi.

A special thank you to Susan for everything great in my life. And thank you to Sophia, Anna and Elanor your support and love.

About the author

When I Wear Bob Kaufman's Eyes is Tom Murphy's third full collection of poetry. Murphy is the Corpus Christi 2021-2022 Poet Laureate and is also the *Langdon Review* 2022 Writer-In-Residence. Recent poetry and photography have been in *Poetry is DEAD: An Inclusive Anthology of Deadhead Poetry, Boundless Anthology, MONO, Corpus Christi Writers* 2018-2022, *Journal of Black Mountain College Studies, Ain't Gonna Be Treated This Way: Celebrating Woody Guthrie; Poems of Protest & Resistance; 3lements; Illya's Honey; Nothing Journal, The Langdon Review, The Great American Wise Ass Poetry Anthology,* Red River Review; *Outrage: A Protest Anthology for Injustice in a Post 9/11 World;* 2016 *Texas Poetry Calendar; Beatitude: Golden Anniversary Edition; Centrifuge; Nebula; Strike; Switchgrass Review; Voices de la Luna* and *Windward Review.* Murphy's other books & CDs: *Snake Woman Moon* (El Grito del Lobo Press, 2021), *Pearl* (FlowerSong Press, 2020), *American History* (Slough Press, 2017), co-edited *Stone Renga* (Tail Feather Press, 2017), chapbook, *Horizon to Horizon* (Strike Syndicate, 2015), CD "Live from Del Mar College" (BOW Productions, 2015), and CD "Slams from the Pit" (BOW Productions, 2014). You reach Tom at tom@tommurphywriter.com or view his website at https://tommurphywriter.com

Made in the USA
Monee, IL
27 August 2023

41707936R00056